Trash! Trash! Trash!

By Shelly Nielsen
Illustrated by Terry Boles

Published by Abdo & Daughters, 4940 Viking Drive Suite 622, Edina, Minnesota 55435.

Library bound edition distributed by Rockbottom Books, Pentagon Tower, P.O. Box 36036, Minneapolis, Minnesota 55435.

Edited by Julie Berg

LIBRARY OF CONGRESS CATALOGING-IN-PUBLICATION DATA
Nielsen, Shelly, 1958-
    Trash! Trash! Trash! / written by Shelly Nielsen : [edited by Julie Berg].
       p. cm. -- (Target Earth)
    Summary: Looks at what happens to litter and garbage when recycling is not practiced.
       ISBN 1-56239-192-5 (lib. bdg.)
       1. Litter (Trash) -- Juvenile literature. 2. Recycling (Waste, etc.) -- Juvenile literature. [1. Recycling (Waste). 2. Litter (Trash).] I. Berg, Julie. II Title. III. Series.
    TD813.N54   1993
    363.7'2'8--dc20

                        93-18952
                        CIP

Thanks To The Trees From Which This Recycled Paper Was First Made.

Do you know what the word "recycle" means? It means to save things and reuse them. Recycling is a good way to cut down on the amount of garbage in the world. Help stop pollution of the Earth. Recycle!

On Earth Day, Zoe's recycling talk was a big hit.
"Never throw cans in the trash," she warned.
"Ahhh!" said the crowd.
"We must recycle cans, bottles, and newspaper," she added.
"Ohhh!" sighed the crowd.
"Save our Earth from garbage," Zoe shouted.
"Yaaay!" Everyone cheered as they gave her a standing ovation. Of course, they were already standing up.

Zoe walked home, smiling. "I wowed 'em," she said to herself. Then she hollered to a make-believe crowd: "I'm the recycling captain of the world!"

Zoe pointed at an empty pop can on the ground. "Never, ever, ever throw aluminum cans in the trash," she said. A little boy standing on the corner stared. Zoe blushed, picked up the can, and kept walking.

At first, carrying the can was no trouble. Then, little by little, it became a bother. The can was gritty. It felt sticky. And home was still blocks away.

"What would happen," she said, "if I just set this little old can back on the ground? One can won't matter. People toss garbage every day."

So, with a shrug, Zoe threw the can over her shoulder. *Ka-lunk!*

The can rolled away.

But as it picked up speed, other garbage followed. There was a noisy clank and clatter as cans and bottles knocked together.

Soon there was a big grimy pile of garbage rolling behind the can. "Stop!" shouted Zoe. "Wait!" But the louder she shouted, the faster the garbage moved.

From every direction, garbage was coming! Mountains of rubbish. Towers of trash. Junk everywhere Zoe looked!

There were broken shoelaces, an old earring or two,
cracked baby bottles, and diapers (P.U.!)...

…a scratched bowling ball, someone's tired plaid socks, clocks with dead batteries and no tick-tock, bad news newspapers, rumpled magazines, all kinds of broken machines…

…fast-food bags, styrofoam cups, old toothbrushes, nibbled Pronto Pups, burned white toast, moldy pickle jars, and empty wrappers from candy bars!

Zoe felt dizzy. The world was covered with litter, hidden by junk. It was so piled with trash, it stunk. Everywhere she looked, there was rubbish. And worst of all, the flowers were smashed. The grass was mashed. And the air smelled like—garbage!

And there, on top of this awful hill of trash, was her one tiny, harmless aluminum can.

Zoe climbed over bruised banana peels. She pushed past empty paint cans. She crawled on top of cracked dishes, empty shampoo bottles, and a dented wheelbarrow with a missing wheel. Finally she reached the top of the garbage heap. "GOTCHA!" she yelled and grabbed the can.

Zoe slid to the bottom of the great hill of garbage. "Don't worry," she said. "I'll find you a nice home in a recycling bag." Then she blushed. She had never spoken to an aluminum can before now.

With a tight grasp on the can, she started toward home. Now she didn't smell rotten garbage anymore. The air was fresh and clean. Pink, purple, and yellow flowers bloomed like jewels in the sweet-smelling grass. The garbage had disappeared.

Had she dreamed everything? Zoe kept her grip on the harmless aluminum can. She wasn't taking any chances. At home, she very, very carefully put the can in the recycling bag. The trash disaster was over—thanks to Zoe, the recycling captain.

Do you recycle at home? Sort out the items that could be recycled.

plastic containers (a variety of milk cartons, margarine tubs, household cleaner bottles)

wire hangers   shriveled oranges
old light bulbs   banana peels
dead batteries   telephone directories
paint cans   newspapers
auto parts   aluminum cans
tires   television sets
broken toys   pop bottles

Do you have ideas about ways to reuse the things that can't be recycled?

Give clothes you've outgrown to a friend or thrift shop. Start a compost pile in your backyard for food and yard waste your family throws away. Give an old television set to a fix-up shop.

Does your family recycle? Talk to your parents about recycling at home. You can be the recycling captain. Help sort the cans, bottles, and newspapers. When your friends and neighbors see your recycling plan, will they want to recycle, too?

TARGET EARTH™ COMMITMENT

At Target, we're committed to the environment. We show this commitment not only through our own internal efforts but also through the programs we sponsor in the communities where we do business.

Our commitment to children and the environment began when we became the Founding International Sponsor for Kids for Saving Earth, a non-profit environmental organization for kids. We helped launch the program in 1989 and supported its growth to three-quarters of a million club members in just three years.

Our commitment to children's environmental education led to the development of an environmental curriculum called Target Earth™, aimed at getting kids involved in their education and in their world.

In addition, we worked with Abdo & Daughters Publishing to develop the Target Earth™ Earthmobile, an environmental science library on wheels that can be used in libraries, or rolled from classroom to classroom.

Target believes that the children are our future and the future of our planet. Through education, they will save the world!

Minneapolis-based Target Stores is an upscale discount department store chain of 517 stores in 33 states coast-to-coast, and is the largest division of Dayton Hudson Corporation, one of the nation's leading retailers.